Trees

Lisa Jane Gillespie
Designed by Helen Edmonds

Illustrated by Patrizia Donaera

Additional illustration and design by Sue King, Zoe Wray and John Russell
Reading consultant: Alison Kelly, Roehampton University
Tree consultant: Christine Meakin, The National Arboretum, Westonbirt

Contents

- 3   A leafy world
- 4   Standing tall
- 6   Growing strong
- 8   Food factories
- 10   Types of trees
- 12   Changing seasons
- 14   Fancy flowers
- 16   Tasty treats
- 18   Hanging on
- 20   Tree houses
- 22   Tough trees
- 24   Crawling with life
- 26   Trees in trouble
- 28   Protecting trees
- 30   Glossary
- 31   Websites to visit
- 32   Index

A leafy world

There are many different types of trees. They can be different shapes and sizes.

This large tree is an oak tree.

Standing tall

Trees are tall, woody plants that can live for hundreds of years.

The top of a tree is called the crown.

Leaves grow on the branches.

A spruce tree in Sweden is the oldest tree in the world. It is almost 10,000 years old.

The strong trunk supports the branches. Water travels from the roots through the trunk to the branches.

Bark protects the trunk and branches from cold and damage.

Roots grow deep underground. They hold the tree in the soil and soak up water.

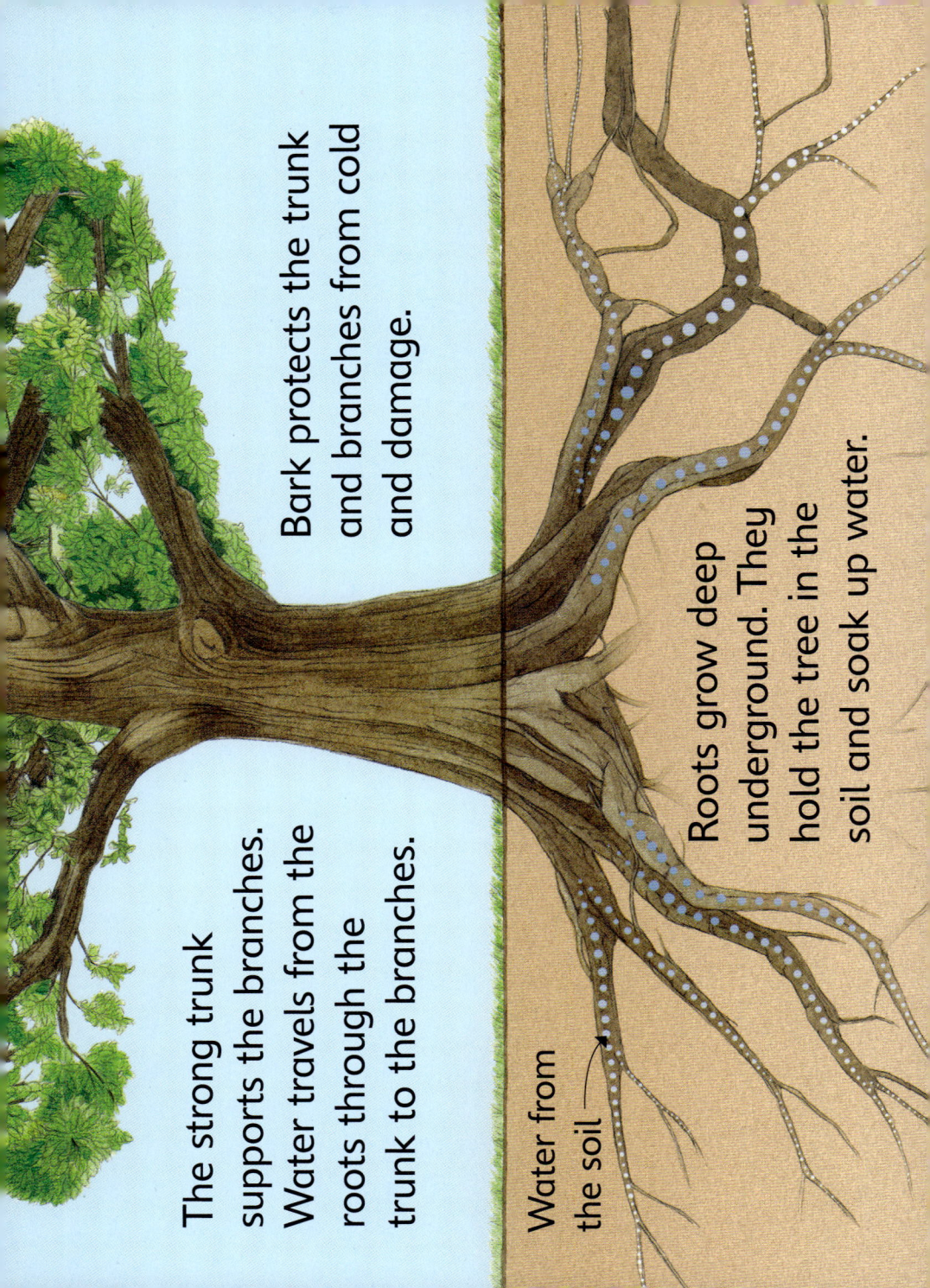

Growing strong

Every tree begins as a tiny seed. In spring, a seed starts to grow.

The first shoot and roots begin to grow from the seed. The roots soak up water.

The shoot grows up to the surface. It becomes a seedling with leaves and buds.

Heat from the Sun and water from the soil help the seedling grow into a sapling.

After many years this green sapling will grow into a tall fir tree.

Food factories

Trees need food to help them grow. The leaves use water, sunlight and air to make food.

Veins

Stem

The stem and veins carry water to the leaf.

Sunlight shines on the leaf.

Air goes into tiny holes on the leaf's underside.

The leaf makes food, and the veins carry it to the rest of the tree. Then, the leaf gives out a gas called oxygen.

Types of trees

There are thousands of different kinds of trees. There are three main tree groups.

Broadleaf trees have bushy crowns with lots of branches.

Evergreen trees are tall and have straight trunks.

Palm trees have bendy trunks with big leaves at the top.

Palm leaves are sometimes called fronds.

This is a sycamore leaf. A sycamore is a broadleaf tree.

These spiky leaves are from an evergreen tree.

Changing seasons

Some broadleaf trees look very different at different times of year.

In summer, the trees are covered with lots of green leaves.

As the weather gets colder the leaves turn orange and red.

The leaves fall to the ground. The branches stay bare all winter.

In spring, new green leaves start to grow on the trees.

Evergreen trees are never bare. They lose their leaves and grow new ones all year long.

When leaves turn orange and red they fall from the branches.

Fancy flowers

Some trees grow flowers in spring. Many flowers attract insects with their smell.

Inside a flower there is a sticky powder called pollen, and a sweet juice called nectar.

Insects drink the nectar and pollen sticks to their bodies.

When the insects
go to another flower
some of the pollen
rubs off.

The tree uses
pollen from
two flowers
to make seeds.

Honey bees do a special dance to
tell each other where to find nectar.

15

Tasty treats

After the flowers die and fall, fruits start to grow. There are seeds inside each fruit.

Hard fruits are called nuts and cones. These dormice are eating a chestnut.

When birds and animals eat the fruits they swallow the seeds.

The seeds are spread by the birds and animals in their droppings.

If the seeds fall on the right soil they grow into new seedlings.

Hanging on

Lots of different plants and mushrooms grow on trees.

Moss is a furry green plant that grows on tree trunks in damp forests.

Mistletoe grows on branches. Its roots suck water and food from the tree.

Orchids grow on rainforest trees. Their roots soak up water from the air.

Velvet foot mushrooms grow in groups on tree trunks.

Jack-o-lantern mushrooms grow at the bottom of trees. They glow a spooky green at night.

Tree houses

Lots of birds and animals make their homes in trees.

Bald eagles build huge nests in very tall trees. The nest is called an eyrie.

Raccoons sleep in holes in trees to stay warm during the cold winter.

Koalas sleep for most of the day in eucalyptus trees. They eat the leaves, too.

This squirrel has made a snug home for its babies in a hollow tree.

Tough trees

All trees need water to survive, but some trees can grow in very dry places.

Argan trees grow in rocky places. Goats climb the trees to eat the leaves because there is no grass.

Jand trees grow in deserts in India. Their long roots reach water far under the ground.

African baobab trees have huge trunks that can store water for the dry, summer months.

Boojum trees grow in dry parts of America. Their wood holds lots of water like a sponge.

Crawling with life

Many bugs live on trees that give them food or protection.

1. A bullhorn acacia tree is home to thousands of ants.

2. They live in the big, hollow thorns of the tree.

3. The ants eat balls of yellow nectar from the leaves.

4. They sting any creatures that might damage the tree.

This sphinx moth has patterns on its body that match the bark of the tree and help it hide from danger.

A tree trunk spider weaves sticky silk on tree bark. The spider pounces on trapped insects.

Trees in trouble

The world's forests are in danger. Trees are being destroyed by fire and people.

Forest fires sometimes start in dry places during very hot weather. This fire in the USA killed thousands of trees.

Trees are chopped down so the wood can be used for fuel and to make paper.

Forests are cleared so land can be used for farming and to build towns or roads.

Even tiny beetles can be dangerous – some carry diseases that kill trees.

Protecting trees

There are lots of ways to save trees for the future.

Used paper can be recycled to make new paper and cardboard. This means that fewer forests are destroyed.

In some forests new trees are planted to replace ones that are chopped down.

Trees are protected in national parks. These trees grow on high, rocky cliffs in the Grand Canyon National Park in the USA.

Glossary

Here are some of the words in this book you might not know. This page tells you what they mean.

 sapling - a young tree.

 broadleaf - a type of tree with a bushy crown and wide, flat leaves.

 evergreen - a type of tree that has leaves all year long.

 rainforest - a tropical forest that grows in hot, rainy places.

 fuel - something that is burned for heat. Wood is a fuel.

 recycling - reusing waste by making new, useful things from it.

 national park - a special park where trees and wildlife are protected.

Websites to visit

You can visit exciting websites to find out more about trees and forests.

To visit these websites, go to the Usborne Quicklinks Website at **www.usborne-quicklinks.com** Read the internet safety guidelines, and then type the keywords "**beginners trees**".

The websites are regularly reviewed and the links in Usborne Quicklinks are updated. However, Usborne Publishing is not responsible, and does not accept liability, for the content or availability of any website other than its own. We recommend that children are supervised while on the internet.

Dragon trees grow in some parts of Africa and Asia. They have a sticky, red liquid inside their trunks that looks like blood.

Index

bark, 5, 25
broadleaf trees, 10, 11, 12, 30
deserts, 23
evergreen trees, 10, 11, 13, 30
flowers, 14-15, 16
forests, 18, 27, 28
forest fires, 26-27
fruit, 16-17
insects, 14-15, 24-25, 27
leaves, 4, 6, 8-9, 10, 11, 12-13, 20, 22
oxygen, 9

mushrooms, 18, 19
national parks, 29, 30
nests, 20-21
paper, 28
rainforests, 18, 30
recycling, 28, 30
roots, 5, 6, 18, 23
saplings, 6-7, 30
seasons, 12-13
seeds, 6, 15, 16-17
seedlings, 6-7, 17
sunlight, 8-9
trunks, 5, 10, 18, 19, 23
veins, 8-9

Acknowledgements

Photo credits

The publishers are grateful to the following for permission to reproduce material: **Cover** © Corbis/Photolibrary; **01** © Jeremy Francis Adobe.com; **02-03** © David Noton/Naturepl; **07** © Roy Morsch/Corbis; **11** (tr) © NHPA/Avalon; **11** (m) © CGTextures; **11** (br) © Keith Rushforth/FLPA; **13** © Jeffrey Conley/Getty Images; **16** © Lothar Lenz/Zefa/Corbis; **17** © Jason Hollefreund/CGTextures; **19** © Mitsuhiko Imamori/Minden Pictures/FLPA; **21** © Sumio Harada/Minden Pictures; **22** © Vincent Leblic/Photononstop/Photolibrary; **25** © Neil Hardwick/Alamy; **26-27** © AlaskaStock/Photolibrary; **28-29** © Jack Dykinga/Naturepl; **31** © Michele Falzone/Alamy.

Every effort has been made to trace and acknowledge ownership of copyright. If any rights have been omitted, the publishers offer to rectify this in any subsequent editions following notification.

First published in 2009 by Usborne Publishing Ltd., Usborne House, 83-85 Saffron Hill, London EC1N 8RT, England. usborne.com Copyright © 2009 Usborne Publishing Ltd. The name Usborne and the devices ⚲ ⚲ are Trade Marks of Usborne Publishing Ltd. All rights reserved. No part of this publication may be reproduced, stored in a retrieval system, or transmitted in any form or by any means, electronic, mechanical, photocopying, recording or otherwise without the prior permission of the publisher. U.E.